Organisms

Contents

Safety in the Science Classroom

Come to class prepared to learn.

Be responsible and stay safe.

- Follow directions.
- Be an alert observer: use eyes to look and ears to listen.
- Put materials away properly.
- Clean up after yourself.
- Throw materials away as directed.
- Tell the teacher if something breaks or spills.
- Ask for help when you need it.
- Report injuries immediately.
- Tell the teacher if you are not sure of procedures.

Be careful at all times.

- Use materials and tools carefully and as directed.
- Use goggles to protect your eyes, if necessary.
- Keep materials away from your mouth.
- Keep hands away from your mouth.
- Pour liquids carefully.
- Smell things by waving your hand over the container toward your nose (wafting). Never put your nose close to any substance to smell it.

Be courteous.

- Speak in a soft voice when others are working.
- Respect others and their need for space.

Organisms

What animals do you see?

What plants do you see?

What other living things do you think might be there that you cannot see?

We're going to learn about many different living things.

Living Things

How can you tell if something is **living** or not? Is a wagon that moves by itself alive? What about a plant that is on a rock in a park?

What is the difference between a plant and an animal? You must have a few ideas. Plants are often green, and many animals move around. But how are they alike?

Let's find out.

Is a duck alive? Is a wagon alive? Is grass alive?

Experience

It's Alive!

Our world is made up of many things.

Some things are living and some things are not living. How do you know something is alive?

Plants and animals are living things. What do they need to stay alive?

How do you know something is alive?

What Living Things Need

What do living things need to live and grow?

They need food.

They need water.

They need air.

They need a place to live.

Experience
Plants and Animals

What animal do you see? What plants do you see?

Do plants and animals need the same basic things to live?

How are plants and animals the same? How are they different?

What animal is this? What plants are these? How are animals and plants the same? How are they different?

Experience

Different Plants, Different Seeds

Name the **seeds** you know. Did you name pumpkin seeds? How about coffee beans?

Look at all the different kinds of seeds.

How are the seeds alike? How are the seeds different?

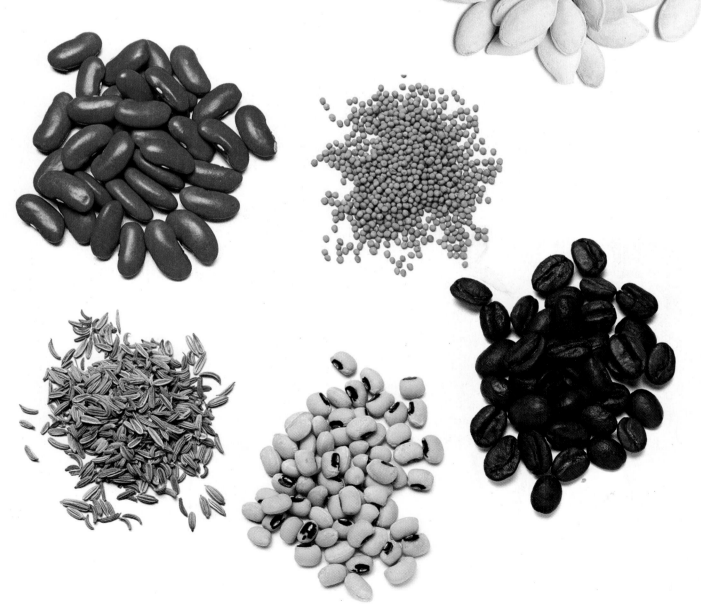

Mr. Camacho helps people grow food.

Biography
Meet Felipe Camacho

Let's meet Felipe Camacho. Mr. Camacho is a community and youth gardens leader. He helped create educational programs at the Sustainable Food Centers in Austin and San Antonio, Texas.

The Sustainable Food Center is a place where fruits and vegetables are grown.

Mr. Camacho studied science in college. He learned how to grow fruits, vegetables, flowers, and other plants.

He learned that all plants begin as seeds. He learned what seeds need to grow into healthy plants.

A Master Gardener

Mr. Camacho is a master gardener. He works at youth gardens and in garden education programs. Mr. Camacho teaches young people what seeds and plants need to survive.

He teaches students to plant seeds in good soil. Mr. Camacho shows students how soil helps seeds grow.

Mr. Camacho also teaches students how much water plants need. If seeds and plants do not get enough water, they will dry up and die. But getting too much water may stop seeds from growing.

Gardeners know how to grow plants.

Serving the Community

Mr. Camacho works in places where people learn how to grow healthy food. He finds places to grow lots of fruits and vegetables. More fruits and vegetables mean more people can enjoy them.

watering can

Tools of the Trade

Watering cans help keep soil moist so that seeds can grow into healthy plants.

Gloves protect hands from pointy plants. Gloves also keep soil from getting under your fingernails.

gloves

A **garden fork** is used to break up and dig in soil.

garden fork

Experience

Observing Seeds

You have learned about seeds. You have observed seeds.

Scientists often make drawings of the things they observe. Let's draw pictures of the seeds you have seen. You can keep drawings in your Science Notebook.

Scientists make drawings of what they see.

Experience

Measuring Plants

A few days ago we planted seeds.

I wonder how much they grew.

Let's measure the plants. Let's see how tall they are now.

How tall is your plant?

Growing Plants

You see plants growing all around you. They are in your backyard and your school yard. They grow outside in window boxes and inside your home.

Have you ever looked closely at different plants? There are things about plants that are the same and things that are different.

Let's look for the ways they are the same and different. Let's compare different plants and draw them.

Have you looked at plants up close?

Experience

Forest and Freshwater Plants

Plants are all around us. They grow in fields, rivers, lakes, oceans, on mountains, and in our own backyards.

Plants in Freshwater

Look at the freshwater pond. These plants are **elodea** and **duckweed.** They are freshwater plants. How are they alike? How are they different?

elodea

Some plants grow in freshwater ponds.

duckweed

Plants in a Forest

Look at the **forest**. These plants are **moss** and **ferns**. They are forest plants. How are they alike? How are they different?

ferns

Some plants grow in forests.

moss

Experience

Make a Terrarium

What are the things that plants need to live and grow?

They need food.

They need water.

They need air.

They need a place to live.

If we build a terrarium, we can provide all these things for plants.

Plants can grow in a terrarium.

Pumpkins grow along the ground.

Bean plants cling to other plants.

Experience

From Seed to Plant

We are growing pumpkin plants and bean plants.

They are very different.

Pumpkin plants have big leaves and big, orange flowers.

Bean plants grow and climb on other plants. Some are even bushy.

They make beans and pumpkins. It's fun to watch them grow.

Parts of a Plant

Do you remember the parts of a plant?

Point to the leaves.

Point to the stem.

Point to the roots.

Point to the seed cover.

Checkpoint

Review

You have spent the past two weeks studying plants and even growing your own plants.

Let's review what you have learned.

What do these plants need to grow?

What do plants need to grow?

Seeds

Where are the seeds in this apple? What are the apple's seeds for?

Where are the seeds?

Living or Not Living?

You have observed things that are living and things that were never living.

Which of these are living?

Compare the Plants

Look at these plants.

What do you observe?

Name something that is different between the plants.

Plant Growth

Below are some pictures that show what happens when a seed is planted. Put the pictures in the correct order. Begin with what happens first and end with what happens last.

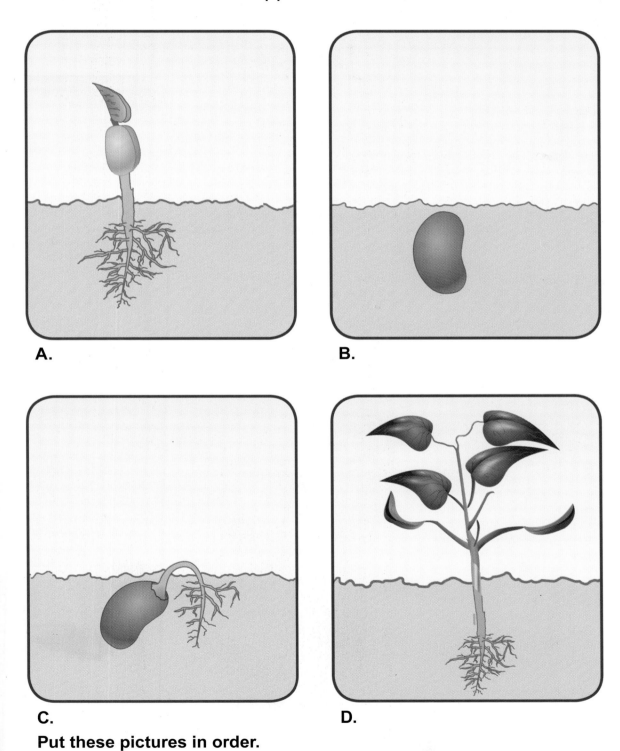

A.

B.

C.

D.

Put these pictures in order.

All About Animals

Think of some animals you know. Have you ever looked at small animals up close?

Think about where animals live. What changes have you seen in an animal's home or their home over time? How has your home changed?

You are going to examine many different animals in this lesson, so start looking at the world around you!

Have you ever looked at animals closely?

Experience

Great Guppies and Super Snails

Have you looked closely at plants and animals that live in water? Have you ever touched a fish? Have you seen a snail?

These animals live in ponds and streams. You're going to build a home for them. Their home is called an **aquarium.**

Then you're going to see how these animals live.

You can build a home for fish and snails.

Can you tell the female guppy from the male?

Which part of the snail is hard? Which parts are soft?

Experience

Water Animal Homes

You have looked at several **guppies** and **snails** over the past few days. Let's see what you can remember about them.

What does a guppy need in its **habitat** to live?

What does a snail need in its **environment** to live?

What do guppies and snails have in common?

Experience

Plenty of Pill Bugs

These are **pill bugs.** What shape are they? What color are they?

What are the body parts of the pill bug? What do you think each body part does?

Pill bugs are often found in groups.

Experience

A Bunch of Beetles

This is a bess beetle. What does a bess beetle look like?

What body parts does a bess beetle have? How does a bess beetle move?

What do bess beetles need to survive?

Can you name the body parts of this bess beetle?

Different Beetles

Look at all these different kinds of **beetles!**

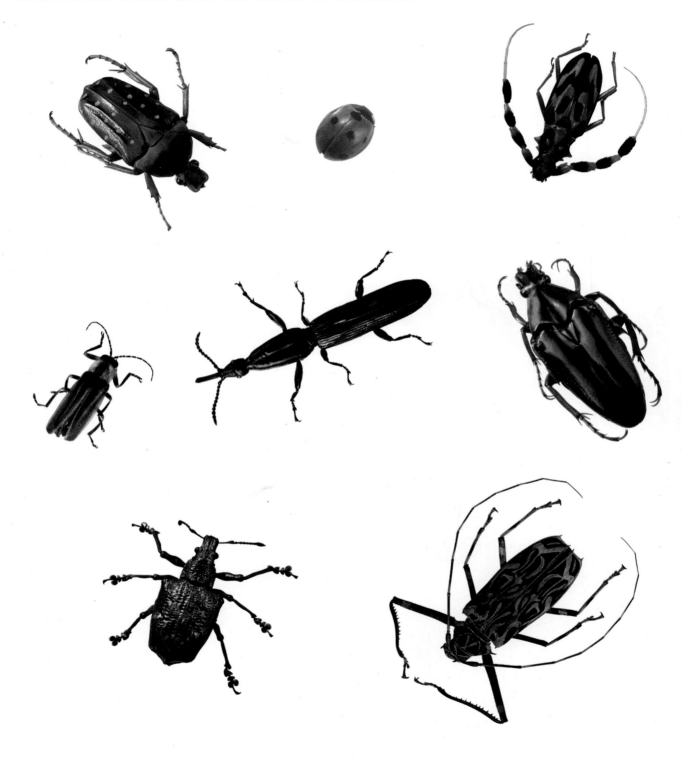

Experience

Many Millipedes

These are **millipedes.** What do they look like?

What body parts does a millipede have? How does the millipede move?

What does a millipede need to survive?

Look at all the legs these millipedes have!

Dr. Young studied at Howard University.

Biography
Meet Dr. Roger Arliner Young

Dr. Roger Arliner Young was a zoologist. A **zoologist** is a scientist who studies animals.

She was born in 1899 and grew up in Pennsylvania. In 1916, she began college at Howard University.

Dr. Young began to study very small animals that live in water. Animals that live in ocean water are called marine animals.

A Good Team

Her teacher was an African American zoologist named Ernest Everett Just. Dr. Just believed that Dr. Young could be an excellent scientist.

Dr. Young and Dr. Just studied how marine animals are different from other animals. They studied what these animals need to live. They also studied the eggs of these animals. They studied how the animals behave in their habitat.

Dr. Young impressed Dr. Just. He called her a "real genius."

Dr. Just thought Dr. Young was a real genius.

Back at Howard University

Dr. Young studied sea urchins. Sea urchins are pointy-shelled animals that live on the ocean floor.

Dr. Young studied the eggs of sea urchins. Dr. Young's work helped doctors understand illnesses like cancer and sickle-cell anemia.

Dr. Young was proud of what she had done. She also wanted to learn more. She decided to go back to school.

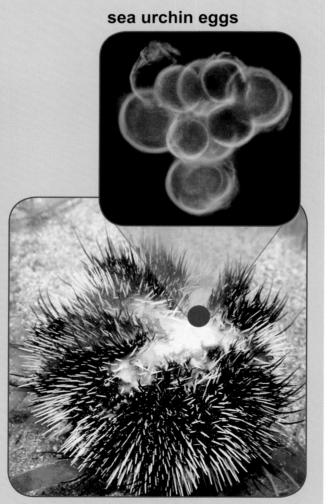

sea urchin eggs

sea urchin

This sea urchin is releasing eggs.

Dr. Young earned a degree from the University of Pennsylvania.

An Important First

In 1940, Dr. Young earned an advanced degree in zoology.

She was the first African American woman to earn an advanced degree in zoology.

Experience
Changes over Time

How have the plants and other living things in the aquarium changed? Were the changes that happened what you expected, or did you expect something different?

Our world does not stay the same. It is always changing over time.

Look at the ground near Mount Saint Helens in 1980.

Look at the same ground 20 years later.

Habitats Change

As you know, seasons change. Spring changes to summer. Beaches also change as the ocean moves sand around. After land has been damaged, plants will grow back over time.

This is a Pennsylvania marsh in summer.

This is the same marsh in winter.

Checkpoint

Review

You have spent the past three weeks studying animals. You have observed the animals and talked about how they are alike and how they are different.

Let's see how much you remember.

Below is a picture of two freshwater snails.

What does a snail need to live?

What Goes in the Aquarium?

Below is a picture of an aquarium.

What does a fish need to live? What things do you need
to add to the aquarium?

Compare the Animals

Below are a millipede and a pill bug.

What is one thing that they have in common?

What is one way that they are different?

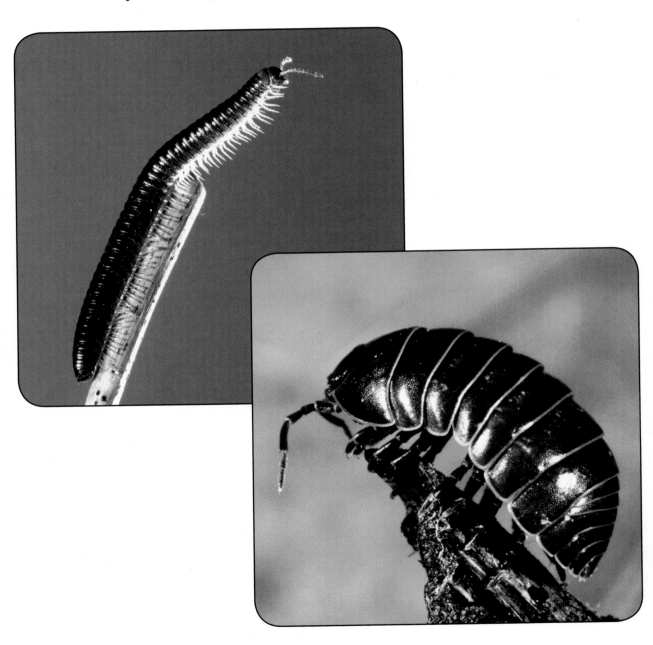

What Do Millipedes Need?

Where do millipedes live?

What are three things that they need to live?

Life in a Terrarium

You have spent some time looking at plants and animals in your terrarium. You have looked at living things like pill bugs and millipedes and ferns and mosses.

But how do these animals compare to other animals? How do these plants compare to other plants? What do living things have in common?

Let's look at life in our terrarium.

Experience

Terrarium Observations

What did you observe about the terrarium?

How has it changed?

How have the plants changed?

Are there more or fewer animals?

What do the plants and animals need to survive in a terrarium?

How has life in your terrarium changed?

Experience
Write About Our Terrarium

You have seen changes in the terrarium. Let's write about what you've seen.

How do these changes compare with those in nature? How are they similar? How are they different?

Write about what you see in the terrarium.

Experience
Observing Plants

Freshwater plants are found in rivers, lakes, streams, and ponds. Freshwater plants like elodea and forest plants like ferns are similar. They are also different.

What did you observe about the freshwater plant? What did you observe about the forest plant?

How are they alike? How are they different?

elodea

ferns

Experience
Comparing Plants

Look at the plants in the forest. What features do they have?

redwood trees

birch trees

Water Plants

Look at the plants in the water. What features do they have?

How are these plants the same? How are they different?

freshwater plants

lily pads and grasses

Experience

What Do Plants Need?

Plants need water, sunlight, air, and a place to live and grow. Most plants live in soil, but some live in water.

Plants use sunlight to make food.

Plants need water to grow.

Plants need air.

Plants need a place to live.

Dr. Sanchez studies how soil and plants act on each other.

Biography
Meet Dr. Pedro Sanchez

Dr. Pedro Sanchez is a soil scientist. He studies soil in order to make crops grow better. Dr. Sanchez's work results in healthier plants for people around the world to eat.

Dr. Sanchez has always been interested in soil and plants. He says, "I used to like to play in the dirt on my dad's farm. I loved being on the farm and I liked soil."

The Needs of Corn

Dr. Sanchez has to know what plants like corn need. Corn grows better when it is planted near peas. Other plants can help corn grow better.

Dr. Sanchez teaches people how other plants can help corn grow.

Mr. Sanchez knows what helps corn grow.

Mr. Sanchez's writings help people grow better plants for us.

Helping Everyone

Dr. Sanchez has written a book and more than 200 articles about helping plants grow. His work is important to scientists and to us.

Scientists use what they learn from Dr. Sanchez to help people such as farmers grow better plants. When plants grow better, they produce more food for everyone. Dr. Sanchez helps everyone.

Experience
Different Homes

What did the plants and animals in the terrarium and aquarium have in common?

Why do you think those features were the same?

What was different about the plants and animals?

Is it possible to switch the animals in the terrarium and aquarium?

Is it possible to switch the plants in the terrarium and aquarium?

Focus

Organisms Everywhere

You have been learning about many different plants and animals. You have seen many living things. Living things are called **organisms.**

Animals are organisms. Plants are organisms, too.

What organisms do you see in this picture?

Animals

Some animals live on land, and some animals live in the water.

But what do all of those animals need to survive?

They need food, air, water, and a habitat.

Living things, big or small, need these things. All organisms need these things.

Some animals live on land.

Some animals live underground.

Some animals live in the water.

pill bugs

millipedes

elephant

cheetah

wolf

Canada geese

Land Animals

Some animals live on the land.

They need to breathe the same air that you breathe. They do not live in the water.

Think about the millipedes and pill bugs we looked at a few weeks ago. These animals live only on the land.

The millipedes and pill bugs live, eat, sleep, and drink on land. They can get everything they need to live and grow on land.

Can you think of other animals that live on land?

Lots of fish!

stingray

sea star

lionfish

harlequin turkfish

queen triggerfish

Water Animals

Some animals live in water. If a fish were on land, it would flop around, gasping for air. It would not survive on land.

But fish, too, can find air to breathe, food to eat, water to drink, and places where they can be safe and grow.

It is a very different place from the land, but animals such as fish are at home in underwater conditions. Some animals live only in water.

Land Plants

Some animals can live only on land. Some plants can live only on land, too.

Think about the plants in your backyard, neighborhood, or school yard. Chances are you have seen bushes, grass, and trees such as pines, maples, or oaks. These are land plants. They can live only on land.

If these plants were placed in the water, they would not survive. The roots of a land plant can be very deep. Plants have to reach deep into the soil to get the water they need to survive. There is too much water in a lake or stream for these plants to live.

grass

apple tree

palm tree

redwood trees

vines

roses

cattails

water lilies

elodea

duckweed

Water Plants

Some plants grow only in very wet or swampy places. These plants are water plants.

Have you ever seen a water lily? This kind of lily can live only in the water. Water lilies have a large leaf that floats on the surface of a pond or a lake and a stem that reaches to the bottom. These plants would not survive on land.

You also looked at elodea in this science lesson. You saw that this plant is small, light green, and thin. This plant also lives in the water.

Think About It

What do all plants need to live?

What do all animals need to live?

What does a dog need to live?

What does a tree need to live?

Checkpoint
Review

What are some of the living things in your terrarium?

What are some of the nonliving things in your terrarium?

What did you see in your terrarium?

What Do Plants Need?

What do plants need to live?

Plants have needs. What are they?

Terrarium and Aquarium

Here are a terrarium and an aquarium.

How are these two things alike?

How are they different?

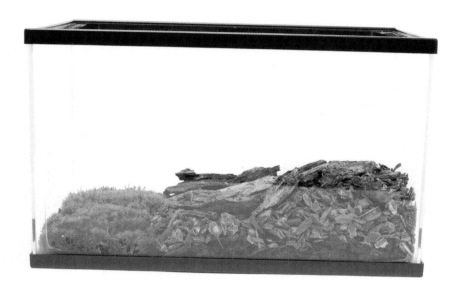

Plants and Animals

Some plants and animals are found only in the water and some are found only on land.

Which of the plants and animals below are found on land? Which are found in the water?

How Are They Different?

What do land animals have that water animals don't have?

What do land plants have that water plants don't have?

What do water animals need to live in the water?

What do water plants need to live in the water?

 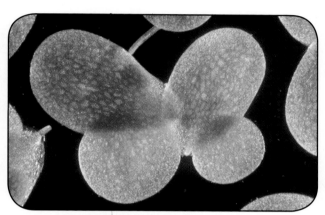

What are the differences between land plants and water plants?

What are the differences between land animals and water animals?

Looking at Life

You have been learning about many different types of animals and plants.

Now it's time to think about yourself. Humans are living things. Humans are organisms and have basic needs.

Humans are animals and share many things with other animals. But humans are also similar to plants. How are we the same? How are we different?

Humans are organisms, too.

Experience
We Are All Special

People are alike and people are different.

Everyone is special.

What makes you special?

What makes each of us special?

Experience

How Do We Compare?

Are we more like plants or animals?

How are we like other animals? How are humans like bess beetles? How are we like guppies? How are we different from other animals?

How are we like plants? How are humans like elodea? How are humans like ferns? How are humans different from plants?

How are we like animals?
How are we like plants?

Checkpoint

Review

What do all people have in common?

How are we the same?

What Do Organisms Need?

What do humans and other organisms need to live?

What do organisms need?

Plants and Animals

How are plants and animals different?

How are plants and animals the same?

What Did You Learn?

You have built a terrarium and an aquarium over the past few weeks.

What did you learn about the animals and plants that live in the terrarium and the aquarium?

Tables of Measure

Length

Metric System	English System
1 centimeter (cm) = 10 millimeters (mm)	1 foot (ft) = 12 inches (in.)
1 decimeter (dm) = 10 centimeters (cm)	1 yard (yd) = 36 inches (in.)
1 meter (m) = 10 decimeters (dm)	1 yard (yd) = 3 feet (ft)
1 meter (m) = 100 centimeters (cm)	1 rod (rd) = 16 ½ feet (ft)
1 decameter (dam) = 10 meters (m)	1 mile (mi) = 5280 feet (ft)
1 kilometer (km) = 1000 meters (m)	1 mile (mi) = 1760 yards (yd)

Weight (Mass)

Metric System	English System
1 gram (g) = 1000 milligrams (mg)	1 pound (lb) = 16 ounces (oz)
1 kilogram (kg) = 1000 grams (g)	1 ton (T) = 2000 pounds (lb)
1 metric ton (t) = 1000 kilograms (kg)	

Capacity

Metric System	English System
1 liter (L) = 1000 milliliters (mL)	1 pint (pt) = 2 cups (c)
1 decaliter (daL) = 10 liters (L)	1 quart (qt) = 2 pints (pt)
1 kiloliter (kL) = 1000 liters (L)	1 gallon (gal) = 4 quarts (qt)
	1 peck (pk) = 8 quarts (qt)
	1 bushel (bu) = 4 pecks (pk)

Useful Measurement Equivalents

Length
1 inch = 2.54 centimeters
1 foot = 12 inches = 30.48 centimeters
1 yard = 3 feet = 36 inches = 91.44 centimeters

Weight (mass)
1 oz = 28.35 grams
1 pound = 16 ounces = 453.59 grams
1 ton = 2000 pounds = 907 kilograms

Volume
1 quart (liquid) = 2 pints = 32 fluid ounces = 946 milliliters (0.946 liter)

Rulers You Can Use

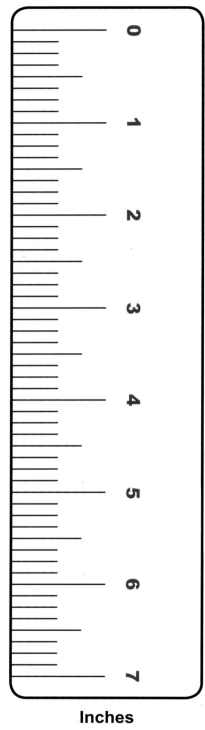

Inches

English System

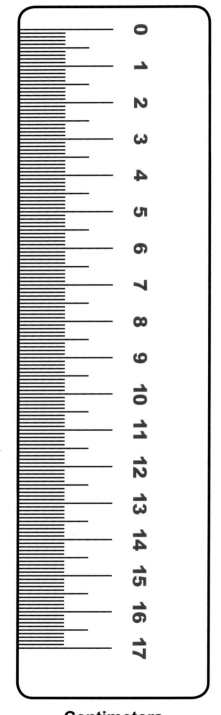

Centimeters

Metric System

Steps in the Scientific Method

Scientific method is a process that scientists follow to explore and find answers to questions.

Question, Purpose, Problem

Hypothesis, Prediction

Materials

Procedures, Experimentation, Investigation

Results, Data

Conclusions

Make Inferences from Conclusions

Communicate Results

Suggested Roles for Students in Cooperative Groups

- **Group Leader** maintains order, keeps efforts focused, facilitates cooperative work, and serves as a timekeeper.

- **Equipment and Materials Manager** gathers, organizes, and returns equipment needed for specific activities.

- **Chief Engineer** or **Chief Scientist** helps the group follow step-by-step instructions for construction activities and demonstrates steps when necessary.

- **Recorder** keeps and writes down important information, including decisions and results, for the group.

Self-Assessment Checklist for Group Work

☐ I remembered my special job (or role).

☐ I was a careful observer.

☐ I followed directions.

☐ I listened to my teammates.

☐ I participated in group discussions.

☐ I was polite and considerate of others.

☐ I completed the work and helped clean up.

Careers in Science

- **Astronomer** – studies the stars, planets, and other heavenly bodies

- **Biochemist** – studies cells to determine the life processes of cells and entire organisms

- **Biologist** – studies life processes of plants and animals

- **Botanist** – studies plants

- **Chemist** – studies the make-up and properties of substances and how they react with one another

- **Civil Engineer** – designs highways, bridges, tunnels, waterworks, harbors, and so on

- **Computer Scientist** – studies and applies computer programming

- **Electrical Engineer** – applies the technology of electricity to the design and operation of equipment

- **Entomologist** – studies insects

- **Geologist** – studies the structure and history of Earth

- **Laboratory Technician** – performs laboratory processes, tests, experiments, and so on

- **Medical Doctor** – practices medicine to treat sickness, injury, and disease

- **Meteorologist** – studies the atmosphere and weather conditions

- **Nurse** – takes care of sick and injured people

- **Oceanographer** – studies the physical properties of the ocean

- **Zoologist** – studies animals

Sample Graphs

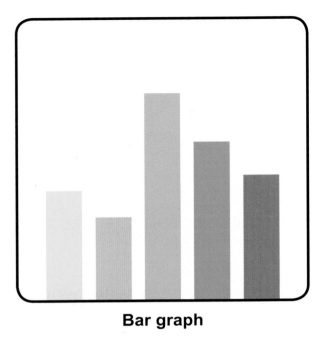

Bar graph

Line graph

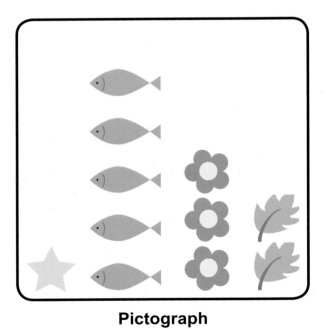

Pictograph

Pie graph

Six Major Groups of Living Things

Animals

Plants

Fungi

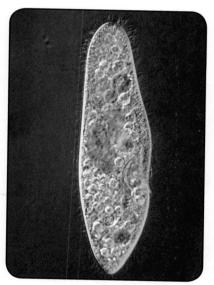

**Protozoa and Algae
(protists)**

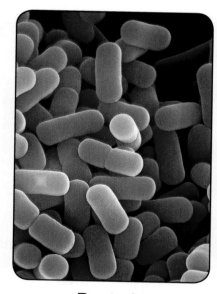

Bacteria

**Extreme Bacteria
(archaebacteria)**

Our World

Living Things

Nonliving Things

Pronunciation Guide

The table below provides sample words to explain the sounds associated with specific letters and letter combinations used in the respellings in this book. For example, *a* represents the short "a" sound in *cat*, while *ay* represents the long "a" sound in *day*. Letter combinations are used to approximate certain more complex sounds. For example, in the respelling of *Celsius*—SEL-see-uhs—the letters *uhs* represent the vowel sound you hear in *shut* and *other*.

Vowels

a	short a: **a**pple, c**a**t
ay	long a: c**a**ne, d**ay**
e, eh	short e: h**e**n, b**e**d
ee	long e: f**ee**d, t**ea**m
i, ih	short i: l**i**p, **a**ct**i**ve
iy	long i: tr**y**, m**igh**t
ah	short o: h**o**t, f**a**ther
oh	long o: h**o**me, thr**ow**
uh	short u: sh**u**t, **o**ther
yoo	long u: **u**nion, c**u**te

Letter Combinations

ch	**ch**in, an**c**ient
sh	**sh**ow, mi**ss**ion
zh	vi**s**ion, a**z**ure
th	**th**in, heal**th**
th	**th**en, hea**th**er
ur	b**ir**d, f**ur**ther, w**or**d
us	b**us**, cr**us**t
or	c**our**t, f**or**mal
ehr	**err**or, c**are**
oo	c**oo**l, tr**ue**, f**ew**, r**u**le
ow	n**ow**, **ou**t
ou	l**oo**k, p**u**ll, w**ou**ld
oy	c**oi**n, t**oy**
aw	s**aw**, m**au**l, f**a**ll
ng	so**ng**, fi**ng**er
air	**A**ristotle, b**a**rrister
ahr	c**ar**t, m**ar**tyr

Consonants

b	**b**utter, **b**a**b**y
d	**d**og, cra**d**le
f	**f**un, **ph**one
g	**g**rade, an**g**le
h	**h**at, a**h**ead
j	**j**u**dg**e, gor**g**e
k	**k**ite, **c**ar, bla**ck**
l	**l**ily, mi**l**e
m	**m**om, ca**m**el
n	**n**ext, ca**nd**id
p	**p**rice, co**pp**er
r	**r**ubber, f**r**ee
s	**s**mall, **c**ircle, ha**ss**le
t	**t**on, po**tt**ery
v	**v**ase, **v**i**v**id
w	**w**all, a**w**ay
y	**y**ellow, ka**y**ak
z	**z**ebra, ha**z**e

Glossary

aquarium: a tank, pool, or bowl filled with water for keeping live fish, underwater animals, and plants

beetle: any of a large number of insects with wing covers that meet in a straight line

dead: no longer living, no longer able to grow and breathe

duckweed: a small freshwater plant that lives on the surface of the water

elodea: a freshwater plant that often lives underwater

environment: all surroundings that affect the life of a living thing

fern: a forest plant that likes warm, wet areas

forest: land that is covered by trees and shrubs

guppy: a small, live-bearing freshwater fish found in parts of Central and South America and the Caribbean

habitat: a place where a plant or animal normally lives

living: alive, able to grow and breathe

marine animal: an animal that lives in ocean water

master gardener: a person who has studied and become an expert on fruits, vegetables, flowers, and other plants

measure: to use a ruler to see how tall something is

millipede: an animal with 20 to more than 100 segments with two pairs of legs on each segment

moss: a tiny green plant that does not flower

nonliving: never alive, never able to grow and breathe

organism: a living thing

pill bug: a small animal with seven sections, each with a pair of legs, that can curl itself into a ball

seed: the part of a plant that can grow into a new plant

snail: a soft-bodied animal that usually forms a shell that protects most of its body

survive: to stay alive

terrarium: a clear, covered container with small plants and other living things inside

window box: a container that sits on a window sill that holds soil and plants

zoologist: a scientist who studies animals

Illustrations Credits

Key: t=top; b=bottom; c=center; l=left; r=right

All artwork: © K12 Inc.

Front cover: © Daniel Bosler/Stone/ Getty Images, Inc.; (background) © VStock, LLC/Index Stock.

Back cover: (t) © John Mitchell/Photo Researchers, Inc.; (b) © Brand X Pictures/Jupiterimages.

Introduction: © Gabriela Staebler/ zefa/Corbis

Lesson 1: 3 © Julie Habel/Corbis. **4** © Ariel Skelley/Corbis. **5** (tl) © Royalty-Free/Corbis; (tr) © AGB Photo/Alamy; (bl) © Design Pics/ Punchstock; (br) © Greatstock Photographic Library/Alamy. **6** © AbleStock/Index Stock. **7** (all) © photolibrary/Index Stock. **8** © Lynda Richardson/Corbis; (inset) Courtesy of Ruth Lauer/Sustainable Food Center. **9** © Photodisc/Getty Images, Inc. **10** (t)(c) © Royalty-Free/ Corbis; (b) © Photodisc. **11** © Royalty-Free/Corbis. **12** (c) Yoav Levy/Phototake.

Lesson 2: 13 © Brand X Pictures/ Jupiterimages. **14** © Bates Littlehales/ Animals Animals; (inset, t) © Bernard Wittich/Visuals Unlimited; (inset, b) © George Bernard/Animals Animals. **15** © Royalty-Free/Corbis; (inset, t) © Royalty-Free/Corbis; (inset, b) © Doug Sokell/Visuals Unlimited. **16** © Dave Nagel/The Image Bank/ Getty Images, Inc. **17** (l) © Patti Murray/ Animals Animals; (r) © Evan Sklar/ Botanica/Jupiterimages. **18** © Wally Eberhart/Visuals Unlimited. **19** © Robert Maass/Corbis. **20** © Isabelle Rozenbaum/ Jupiterimages. **21** (tl)(tc)(tr)(bl) © photolibrary/Index Stock; (bc) © K12 Inc.; (br) © Photodisc. **22** (both) © Royalty-Free/Corbis.

Lesson 3: 25 © Steve Satushek/ Botanica/Jupiterimages. **26** © Gregory K. Scott/Photo Researchers, Inc. **27** (l) © Dr. Paul Zahl/Photo Researchers, Inc.; (r) © K12 Inc. **28** © Bill Beatty/Visuals Unlimited. **29** © Scott Camazine/Photo

Researchers, Inc. **30** (all) © Artville. **31** © Wayne Lawler/Ecoscene/Corbis. **32** © Corbis; (inset) Courtesy of the Moorland-Spingarn Research Center/ Howard University Archives. **33** (both) © The Marine Biological Laboratory/ Woods Hole Oceanographic Institution Library. **34** (l) © Flip Nicklin/Minden Pictures; (tr) © Dr. David M. Phillips/ Visuals Unlimited; (br) © Andrew J. Martinez/Photo Researchers, Inc. **35** © From the Collections of the University of Pennsylvania Archives. **36** (t) © Philip James Corwin/Corbis; (b) © Buddy Mays/Corbis. **37** (both) © Michael P. Gadomski/Photo Researchers, Inc. **38** © K12 Inc. **39** (tl) © K12 Inc.; (tc) © PhotoObjects. net; (tr)(bl) © Artville; (cl) © Premium Stock/Jupiterimages; (cr) © Bernard Wittich/Visuals Unlimited; (bc) © Laura Doss/Corbis. **40** (t) © ImageState/ Jupiterimages; (b) © Richard Walters/ Visuals Unlimited. **41** (t) © IT Stock Free; (b) © Artville.

Lesson 4: 43 © BananaStock/ Jupiterimages. **44** © K12 Inc. **45** © Jose Luis Pelaez, Inc./Corbis. **46** (t) © Charles D. Winters/Photo Researchers, Inc.; (b) © Royalty-Free/ Corbis. **47** (both) © Royalty-Free/ Corbis. **48** (t) © John Clegg/SPL/Photo Researchers, Inc.; (b) © Michael P. Gadomski/Photo Researchers, Inc. **49** (tl)(tr) © Royalty-Free/Corbis; (bl) © DesignPics Inc./Index Stock; (br) © photolibrary/Index Stock. **50** © Royalty-Free/Corbis; (inset) © Bruce Gilbert. **51** © Larry Williams/ Corbis. **52** © Stockbyte/Punchstock. **53** (both) © K12 Inc. **54** © Royalty-Free/Corbis. **55** (tl) © Photodisc; (tr) © George D. Lepp/Corbis; (b) © Hans Reinhard/Bruce Coleman, Inc. **56** (tl) © Bill Beatty/Visuals Unlimited; (tc) © Wayne Lawler/Ecoscene/Corbis; (tr)(bl)(bc)(br) © Photodisc. **57** (tl) © Royalty-Free/Corbis; (tc) © DesignPics Inc./Index Stock; (tr)(bl)(bc)(br) © Creatas Images. **58** (tl) © Fabio Cardoso/zefa/Corbis; (tc)(tr)(bl) © Royalty-Free/Corbis; (bc) © Keith Levit Photography/Index Stock; (br) © AbleStock/Index Stock. **59** (tl) © Layne Kennedy/Corbis;

(tr) © Royalty-Free/Corbis; (bl) © Charles D. Winters/Photo Researchers, Inc.; (br) © Bates Littlehales/Animals Animals. **60** (t) © Able Stock/Index Stock; (b) © Royalty-Free/Corbis. **61** © K12 Inc. **62** © Royalty-Free/Corbis. **63** (both) © K12 Inc. **64** (tl) © Able Stock/Index Stock; (tc) © Evan Sklar/Botanica/ Jupiterimages; (tr)(c) © photolibrary/ Index Stock; (cl) © Adam Jones/Visuals Unlimited; (cr) © Dr. Paul Zahl/Photo Researchers, Inc.; (bl) © Paul Bricknell/ Dorling Kindersley; (bc) © Royalty-Free/ Corbis; (br) © K12 Inc. **65** (tl) © Royalty-Free/Corbis; (tr) © George Bernard/ Animals Animals; (bl) © H. Zettl/zefa/ Corbis; (br) © Hans Reinhard/Bruce Coleman, Inc.

Lesson 5: 67 © Getty Images, Inc. **68** © Ariel Skelley/Corbis. **69** (t) © Roy Morsch/age fotostock; (b) © Brand X Pictures/Jupiterimages. **70** (tl) © blickwinkel/Alamy; (tc) © Bill Lyons/ Alamy; (tr) © BananaStock; (cl)(c)(cr) © Comstock Images; (bl) © Pete Leonard/zefa/Corbis; (bc) © Michael Pole/Corbis; (br) © Creatas Images. **71** © Eyewire/Getty Images, Inc. **72** (tl)(bl)(r) © photolibrary/Index Stock; (cl) © Photodisc; (c) © Hot Ideas/Index Stock. **73** (both) © K12 Inc.

Appendix G: (tl) © Dynamic Graphics; (tc) © Photodisc; (tr) © IT Stock; (bl) © Michael Abbey/Visuals Unlimited; (bc) © Dr. Dennis Kunkel/Visuals Unlimited; (br) © Ralph Robinson/ Visuals Unlimited.

Appendix H: (t) NASA Goddard Space Flight Center Image by Reto Stöckli. **Living Things** (tl) © Dynamic Graphics; (tc) © Photodisc; (tr) © IT Stock; (bl) © Michael Abbey/Visuals Unlimited; (bc) © Dr. Dennis Kunkel/Visuals Unlimited; (br) © Ralph Robinson/ Visuals Unlimited; **Nonliving Things** (tl) © Comstock Images/Punchstock; (tc) © photolibrary/Index Stock; (tr) © Matt Meadows/Peter Arnold, Inc.; (bl) © Dynamic Graphics; (bc) © photolibrary/Index Stock; (br) © Brand X Pictures/Jupiterimages.

Index

N

needs of living things, 5, 16, 27, 29, 31, 39, 71
  plants, 6, 16, 19, 49, 60, 62
nonliving things, 3, 4, 21, 61

O

organisms, 54
  See also animals; living things; plants

P

pill bugs, 28, 40, 56
plants
  elodea, 14, 46, 59
  growing, 13–23
  measuring, 12
  needs of, 6, 16, 19, 49, 60, 62
  observing and comparing, 46–48
  parts of, 18
  review and assessment, 19–23, 38, 61–65
  See also seeds
plants, freshwater, 14, 46, 48
plants, land, 58, 64–65, 73
plants, water, 59, 64–65, 73
pumpkin plants, 17

S

Sanchez, Dr. Pedro, 50–52
seeds, 7
  drawing, 11
  planting and growing, 23
seeds, apple, 20
snails, 26
  environment, 27, 38
soil scientist, 50–52

T

terrariums
  as a habitat, 53, 63
  making, 16
  observing, 43–45
  review and assessment, 73
  writing about, 45
Tools of the Trade, 10

Y

Young, Dr. Roger Arliner, 32–35

Z

zoologist, 32–35